Scorpio

THIS BOOK BELONGS TO:

_____

THE WONDERFUL WORLD OF ZODIACS

♏ SCORPIO ♏

Mimi Jones

Dedicated to my daughter, Melly.

All rights reserved.
No part of this book may be reproduced in any form or by any means, electronic or mechanical, and no photocopying or recording, unless you have written permission from the author.

ISBN 978-1-958985-55-7

Text copyright © 2025 by Mimi Jones

www.joeysavestheday.com

A Mimi Book

WELCOME TO: THE WONDERFUL WORLD OF ZODIACS

SCORPIO

Mimi Jones

Dates:

Scorpio spans from October 23 to November 21.

♏ Ruling Planet: ♏

Pluto and Mars rule Scorpio.

Symbol:
The Scorpion represents Scorpio.

Scorpio

Personality:

Scorpios are known for being passionate and resourceful.

Chase your Passion

Strength:

They are very determined and intuitive.

STAY DETERMINED!

TOP SECRET

Weakness:

Scorpios can be secretive and possessive.

Scorpio

Color:

Their lucky colors are deep red and black.

Lucky Numbers:

8, 11, 18, and 22 are lucky for Scorpios.

Compatibility:

Scorpio gets along well with Cancer, Pisces, Virgo, and Capricorn.

CANCER

PISCES

VIRGO

CAPRICORN

Likes:

Scorpios love truth, ambition, and deep connections.

Career:

They excel in careers that require focus and strategic thinking.

Motto:

Their motto is "I transform."

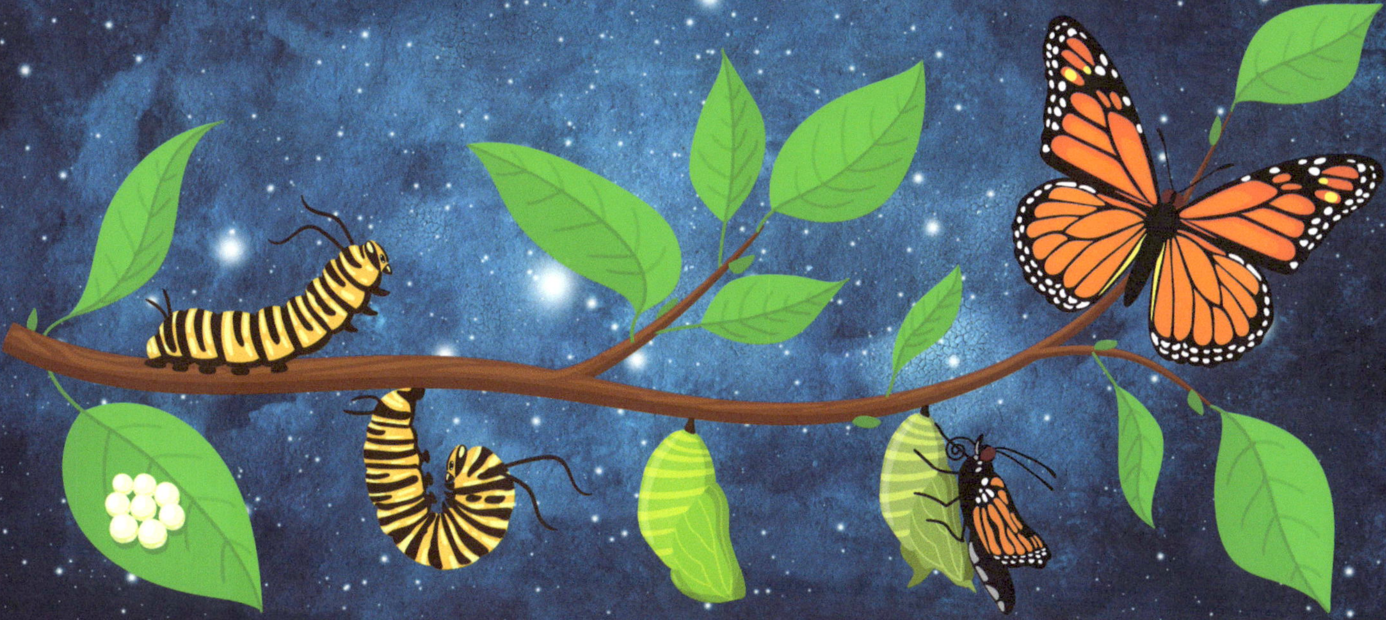

CHANGE

Favorite Day:

Tuesday is their favorite day.

TUESDAY

Health:

Scorpios should take care of their reproductive system and their mental health.

Hobbies:

They enjoy researching, meditating, and uncovering mysteries.

Challenges:

Scorpios need to learn to trust and let go of grudges.

SCORPIO

Influence: They inspire others with their determination and resilience.

Make it **HAPPEN**

**I AM STRONG
I AM CAPABLE
I AM RESILIENT**

Favorite Activities:

Scorpios love activities that involve uncovering secrets or achieving mastery.

Reveal the Secrets

Birthstones:

Topaz and garnet.

If this Zodiac gem tickled your celestial fancy, then you're in for a treat! Dive into my other Zodiac delights right here:

www.mimibooks.com

THE END!

www.ingramcontent.com/pod-product-compliance
Lightning Source LLC
Chambersburg PA
CBHW040030050426
42453CB00002B/69